Deconstruction

Jasmine Whisonant

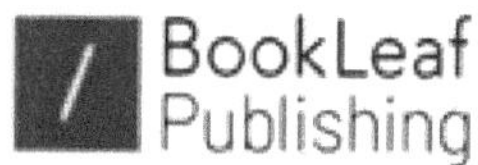

Presentation by *BookLeaf Publishing*

Web: www.bookleafpub.com

E-mail: info@bookleafpub.com

ISBN : 9789357210898

First edition 2022

To those who didn't leave through the breaking,
I will love you until there is not a single trace of
breath in my lungs. Nip, Monet, Shelton, Alani,
Timothy, Jeremiah, Jerwayne, LaShonda, and
Sam.

PREFACE

In the year 2020 I almost renounced my entire
faith. It seemed weightless during a time I
needed to be anchored. Luckily I found God in
the most unconventional ways and although it
was one of the most frightening times of my
existence, I am glad I lived through it. Love is
all I've ever believed in and thank goodness God
is love.

Belonging

Maybe we will meet love like newborns meet their mothers for the first time outside the womb. Maybe it will be met in eyes that remind us of wholeness. Maybe, just maybe, when it comes we know that it belongs to us.

Rescued

You knew me in a way that made coping easy. I didn't have to spill out words to explain my brokenness. I didn't have to conjure up a reason for wanting, you just effortlessly gave. Those golden eyes that you dared me to stare into reminded me that God was alive. My love, I'm not sure where you carried my heaviness. All I know is that everything I've ever crumbled beneath was no longer breaking my fragile heart when you were near.

Safe Space

If an individual behaves recklessly in the space
I've created for them, I think about how freeing
it must be to live recklessly and still be loved.

Worthy

The stars wouldn't tell me what they saw you do last night. The sun told me that even though you rejected the moonlight you were still worth shining on the next morning. Wake up believing there is new grace for you, that the mercy in-store is excited to greet you. This mercy and this grace you've never met before, be excited to greet them too.

The Whole Thing

I don't want to know you only in part. I've known fragments of happiness my entire life. I want the full picture. Even if the canvas is too heavy to carry, I'll find a way. I want to know what color you spill when you come undone and the kind of love you need to be put back together. I want to know you whole and alive and smiling when you think I'm not watching. I want to capture the delight in your eyes when you're talking about your favorite subject. I want you to trust me with your trembling voice when you talk about things that hurt you. I will keep us both steady in those moments. If I fail, you'll know I tried. It can be bit by bit and segment by segment but I don't want to know you only in part.

Deuteronomy 11:14

When the garden in your soul feels like it's a desert and you find that there is no one around to water you, just know that God will send rain. I promise.

The Poem of Gomer

I ain't ever had no love like His
Love that transcends all my wicked
Love that purifies all my messes
All my ick and all my yuck
Like permanent ink spilled on a page
Love like His permanently cleans it up
Ain't ever felt not rush like Gold
No rush like running water in my soul
Especially when He knows
He knows I play the Harlot
He knows I make worry my idol and I commit
adultery with all my anxiety
I cling to my fear and lay close to my
insecurities
He knows I turned away and I sought love in
other places
Came back with the scent of another lover on
my neck
Came back with jewelry he didn't purchase
draped around my wrist
I ain't ever had no love like His
I ain't ever had no love like diamonds
No love like its strong covalent bonding
Ain't ever seen no heart drip mercy like faucet
Like falling
Like flying

Like picking up what's fallen
Ain't ever had no love like this
Love that lures me in the desert speaks tenderly
and still tells me I am His
Ain't ever felt no grace like warm skin
No grace like soft hands
No love like the Songs of Solomon
No love that says I'll be husband
Ain't ever heard no voice call me bride
No voice that reminds me of our covenant in the
night
Ain't ever had no love like light
No love like right
No love like life
Ain't ever felt no life like love
Ain't ever had no love give life

Honestly

Ain't ever had no life until I found His love
Ain't ever had no love like His

A Message for the Broken

Why have we become so infatuated with other people tearing down our walls? Do we view them as more loving when they are bloody? Is it easier to trust them because we are the cause of their scars yet they are still accessible to us? When will we know love at first glance and embrace it without a second look? Not because of its feeling but its action. When will we do the hard work to make our territory safe for those deserving to come in? Hopefully, we learn to accept love well before it's exhausted. Hopefully, we learn to accept people far before they drown in their own tears trying to get through to us.

Keep On

It will all make sense
Just keep living your life child
It will all make sense

Strings and Percussion

I loved you like symphonies
I don't believe you are too young to know what
melodies sound like
I prayed for you every day in your mother's
womb
My voice was violin to God's ears
I just wanted you to be healthy
I wanted you to be the little girl your parents
asked for
But you were bold enough to surprise us
You were bold enough to be a drum when we
expected piano chords
When I held you for the first time I knew that
your cries were crescendos that forced me to be
softened
I knew what it was like to melt
I knew what it was like to be molded again
I wiped the sweat from your brows when you
were hot
I laid blankets on your back when you were cold
and not strong enough to cover yourself
Mama said, "Go lay him down," I said, "he's fine
right here with me"
I remember being too scared to fall asleep
Just to make sure I could hear the flute in your
chest breath

I breathed easy with you in my arms
But I also cried tears in your curls and tried to
wipe them away so you didn't wake up knowing
what pain felt like
I held you tight like you were Cleo
You played the strings on the harp in my chest
and you fell asleep with your ear placed against
your own masterpiece
As you grew older you just kept on amazing me
You had me wrapped around your finger I could
have been your wedding ring
I vowed to play baseball when you wanted me to
I played hide and seek determined to never go
too far so that you would remember that you
could always find me
4 years old I still carried you around malls and
grocery stores
Your parents convinced that you were being lazy
but I considered the weight of your body like
bass
and I considered myself a bass player
5 years old you started throwing tantrums
I remember feeling like you threw away the ring
I gave
I remember thinking my score for love stories
morphed into scores for horror scenes
You were a little more entitled now

I remember the first time I told you no, you
threw a bag of marshmallows on the ground and
you screamed at the top of your lungs
Truth is, I wanted to give you the snack but
more than that...
I wanted you to know that love still covers even
when you're mad
I spent that entire summer trying to convince
myself that God's love still covers even when
I'm sad

The next morning you came into the room and
whispered my name
Your voice reminded me of redemption
Your sweet face reminded me that joy is like the
sun, bright and unfailing
Your smile was my reminder that my life had a
composer
When pain made a home in my soul
When sin played tug a war with my emotions
When fear broke from the inside of my courage
God was still my composer
He perfected me through failed rehearsals
He corrected me when I lived my life off-key
He loved me when I couldn't keep the rhythm
because I couldn't hear the beat

6 years old I've been away for a while and you
run to hug me
7 years old you ask me when I'm coming back to
stay and why I've been gone so long
8 years old you wrap your arms around my torso
8 years old you remind me of drums
You remind me of heartbeats

9 years old I missed your birthday and it
reminded me that I still love you like
symphonies

And my precious baby brother
You are the reason that I believe that through all
of my emotional tantrums towards God, He still
loves me like symphonies

These Precious Lungs

I'm often unaware that I am not breathing
underwater because our hands are so tightly held
together
It feels like it was always supposed to be this
way
Like your touch was all the oxygen I needed to
survive a drowning soul
It seems so much easier to drown in our secrets
than to gasp for air after being restricted for so
many lifetimes
But my power, my striving deliverance comes
from knowing just how valuable my lungs are

And no matter how brave we appear in the ocean
these precious precious lungs were not made for
water.

Unrecognizable: Part 1

Frightening is the best way to describe it
I tugged my bones out of bed, stood straight up
through the snapping, turned on the light, and
didn't know who the girl was in the mirror
I put my hands on my own chest and it felt like
someone else's heart was beating
My voice settled into a lower register when I
was only familiar with my high pitched bubbly
tone
The sound made my ears feel different
Felt almost as if they were broken
Made me wonder if I'd shoved the Q-Tip too far
and broke something the day before
Frightened that I couldn't hear anymore
Didn't know if I ever knew what God sounded
like
Scholars told me choosing to deconstruct my
faith was spiritual maturity but my faith fell
apart on accident
It wasn't something I had planned
It wasn't something I prepared my soul for like
pastors prepare sermons
Or fiances prepare their wedding vows
I was blind sided
Nothing made sense to me and I'd convinced
myself that nothing ever did

Jesus was just as unfamiliar as I was staring at
me in the mirror

Unrecognizable: Part 2

My hands were not the same color I remembered
them
Like they had been scorched by flames
Like I made a decision to live in the hell I was
now destined for
My desires were different
They didn't reflect the blood wash that I trusted
made me clean
I wasn't white as snow as I recalled but I was
stained
It felt as if this blood wasn't supposed to be on
my skin
Like Jesus wanted me tainted and not pure
Like all the pastors I'd ever had wanted me
controlled and not liberated
The ground kept crumbling and my religious
earth continued to shatter
I turned off the lights to turn them back on and
still
I had no idea who I was

Come Thou Fount

Rushing water is the sound coming from the
depth of my core.
Crying from the inside out is a revealing
experience of just how dependent I am.
How much of my soul I can't keep from
wandering.
How much of me I have little control over.
Needing God doesn't come from a willingness to
want.
It's the fundamental design of who I was created
to be.
No matter how much a captain I want to be, I
know I am not my own creator.
This ship does not belong to me.
I am well aware that the pain that wrecks my
very being when I've drifted too far away, is pain
that is saddled to my spiritual existence.
Pain that separates me from an unbeliever.
I don't have the blessed choice to "not believe".
I've tried.
There is something beautifully pathetic about a
heart that is bound on purpose.

Lesson Number 1

Conditioned to make friends with the end of the cliff
Never brave enough to spread my wings
You so patiently taught me how to fly
I didn't soar immediately but you waited at the bottom and walked me back up every time I failed
Put ointment on my scars and told me to try again
Smiled every time I looked back as I inched closer and closer to the edge
Showed me the best way to gain my momentum
When we walked up for about the 5th time you told me of all the places we'd go
You shared how much excitement you'd find in having a flying partner

You eventually stopped walking me up
Told me you'd always still be at the bottom if I fell
Still smiled and told me how free we would be flying so high together
Convinced me that it would be oh so soon

I quickly noticed I started smiling more than you
I started falling on purpose just to see you

I learned how to fly and pretended I still needed
you
You finally told me big girls could do it on their
own
You stopped smiling altogether
One day I could no longer find you at the bottom

I've spent some time blaming you for me being
broken-hearted but as this thick air upholds my
wings I realize,

I am actually flying.

So thank you is all I have to say!

Mount of Olives

I had to meet Him in the garden when His own
will was low like anchor in the ocean.
He seemed to be truly human there.

To view, the Majestic overwhelmed and aching
was no sight of a joyous celebration.

I had always known Him hero in the streets of
Jerusalem.
He performed miracles that brought hope to a
tangible resurrection.
He was a wonderful power that brought
closeness to healing and wholeness.

But the garden

The garden provided a revelation of a hero's
anguish.
I felt that we both had cups.
I begged Him to take mine.
He asked God to take His.

I stood back and I watched as the angel gave
Him a thirst to drink the will of His father.

It was then that my own strength was manifested in each sip.

Each hard swallow was my reminder that this thorn in my side will be drenched in grace forever.

Jesus sweating in that garden was the first time His blood was shed for me.

To see my divine savior suffering from a human experience that he didn't want to be is my current hope that even on the worst days of my temptation, I will always have the strength to utter the words, "Not my will".

I had to meet Him in the Garden.

I'm the Girl

I'm the girl that sleeps more than 8 hours a day because something keeps whispering rest a little more.

I'm the girl who tries to shove anxiety in a mason jar hoping I twisted the lid too tight to come off.

I enjoy being alone so I don't give much time to people yet I always find that I am giving so much of myself.

I never notice stretching thin to see people happy because I want nothing more than for others to be happy.

I listen to people who don't share the same values as me because I question, who else will?

I'm a homebody. I like my sofa and all my blankets.

I like to laugh until my stomach hurts because it feels so much better than crying. I cry when I can't help it.

I use to get mad at myself for doing so but now I think of how great a laugh will follow the tears.

I love people because I want to. Not because of what they bring with them. When they do bring things, good or bad it doesn't impact how much sunshine I find in their eyes.

I'm the girl I've always known. I am tough enough to make it in this cruel world but fragile enough to be broken while doing so.

Unravel

Come undone darling love
Unravel yourself senseless
At this moment your hair is best messy
You can give way to the release
Neither of us has a knife but I see that you are
bleeding
I'll clean you up
I'll bandage you back together
I'll kiss all the scars that are left behind from this
life that has handled you less than gentle
Don't tiptoe around in sadness as if joy doesn't
belong to you
Everything of value belongs to you
Come undone darling love
I'll be right here with my hands cupped
As if you melting into my palms is the only
thing that makes tomorrow worth anticipating.

Note to Self

It's okay that things fall apart
You don't always have to be the one to put them
back together
Even if somehow you influenced the fall
Mistakes are unintentional
Believe that!
You are not evil
You are not malicious
You are human and capable of error
If you can fix it, try
Just don't lose yourself in attempting to put
pieces together to something that would have
eventually fallen on its own
Such is life
That we love
We lose
We win
We get it right
We get it wrong
But if we never grant ourselves forgiveness we
will forfeit the beauty of learning from our
mistakes
Let it go
If it returns reevaluate, maybe you can hold on a
little tighter
If it never does please know

You are human
You will find new things to believe in
Things you should always believe in won't slip
through your fingers
Even if it feels like it
Although you are shaking
God is all the while keeping you steady

Decided

When I don't know what to believe I still sing,
"Jesus loves me this I know, for the bible tells
me so" Selah.

Gratitude

Thank you for allowing this string of words be worthy of the exhaustion of your eyes.